A *Sliver of Light*

–*Meditations*-

Paintings, Poems & Stories

by Sara Drought Nebel

Balboa Press books may be ordered through booksellers or by contacting:

Balboa Press
A Division of Hay House
1663 Liberty Drive
Bloomington, IN 47403
www.balboapress.com
1 (877) 407-4847

ISBN: 978-1-4525-2212-8 (sc)
ISBN: 978-1-4525-2213-5 (e)

Library of Congress Control Number: 2014916364

Printed in the United States of America.

Balboa Press rev. date: 09/26/2014

BALBOA
PRESS
A DIVISION OF HAY HOUSE

THANK YOU

Thank you to all of the Minnows in my life who have helped me to "see". Some, I have known all of my life, some I have recently met, and some have inspired me with their words, songs and brushstrokes from afar, or long after the body who created them, was gone –

James and Lorna Drought, Blake, Cory and Franceska Nebel, Berthold Nebel, Max H. Peters, Anne Kubitsky and the Look for the Good Project, e.e. cummings, Emily Dickinson, Silvia Plath, Henry David Thoreau, E. F. Schumacher, Vincent van Gogh, Edward Hopper, Georgia O'Keeffe, Sacagawea, Rachel Carson, John Muir, Woody Guthrie, Martin Luther King Jr., John Lennon, Stephen Colbert, Gangaji, Dave Matthews and many more... thank you.

☺ Sara Drought Nebel

INTRODUCTION – A SLIVER OF LIGHT

Several years ago, I saw a beautiful black and white photograph of Edward Hopper's Truro, MA studio, with a dramatic sliver of afternoon light on the bare wall, coming in from the open studio door. As I looked at it, I thought about the quiet expressions of light in his paintings. And, the way humans began our perception of time, with sundials and stone structures built precisely to let in a sliver of light designating the equinoxes and the solstices. The way we followed and recorded the predictable patterns of the moon and stars. The way my senses are ignited by the afternoon sun shining on a stone wall, a tree trunk, the tips of tall trees, and cliffs, bathed in orange light as the sun goes down, or through a pink and white shell in the warm sand, or a fallen amber oak leaf, lying humbly on the winter grass, and the silent stories they have to tell.

As I thought about all of these things, I wrote the poem "Awareness". Then recently I read a quote by Hopper that said "I may be mad, but all I ever wanted to do was paint the light as it shines on the side of a building…" I felt so connected with Hopper, the photographer who took that artful photograph, the early peoples who captured the slivers of light in their miraculously built stone time sculptures, and the fleeting light on a leaf or shell. I felt connected to light and time itself, to all artists, to all of life on earth, the moment, the miracle of consciousness, and the power of awareness. I realized that with all of my painting and writing, perhaps this is what I have always unconsciously been trying to express. Awareness, compassion, relationships, the gifts of time and light…. And, that love is the most powerful force on earth.

Awareness

When awareness comes
and words unfold
the ultimate story
of life is told
perhaps
not by words
but might-
be found
in a fleeting
sliver of
light.

☺ Sara Drought Nebel

Plain

Sometimes I am weary of struggle,
for truth that I seek, in this daily juggle.
The simple I strive for is better, I think
than complexity of modern society's "wink".
Skimming the surface of the pretty and mild
conversations, canned, slick and pre-styled-
why not take this route-
handsome décor and snappy suit?
Because that would be dressing an apple as a pear
and I am not comfortable there.
I'm content with my hands in the dirt
wearing a plain, faded sweatshirt
seeing the light as it shines on a tree
speaking plainly, like no one but me.
This way to live is deceptively harder,
living like naked, with no social armor.
But the hurts that will come from the arrows of judgments
are no match for the joy of living with substance.
So, I will worship the sun and lie down and kiss earth
because this, for me, is true worth.
I have answered my question, and although plain is tough
for my words, art and life
plain is more, than enough.

2001

Earthspirit

May my ears hear the music whispering in the wind.
May my eyes see the stories in the shadows
made by wise old trees
on stone walls
in the afternoon.
May my feet feel the message in the rhythm of the waves
on the sand
that began out in the ocean
as the low, rumbling thought
of a magnificent whale
as he dove down
into the emerald secrets of the sea.
May my hands and voice speak the truth
that lies within my soul
so the song of my spirit can join the others
in the wind
in the shadows
and in the sea.
May I be in harmony with earthspirits
everywhere
forever.

1995

"Whale – Sea me" **acrylic on canvas**

Compassion

Everyone is a "me" or an "I".
Everyone who is born will live, and someday, die.
In that flicker of time in between,
everything through his eyes is seen
like no one else who came before
or who will, forever more.
The essence of a soul can rise
to be seen only by another's eyes
and when those eyes meet
face to face
a "spirit bridge" in earthly space
connects us with invisible force
where compassion
can begin its course.

-2001

The Underwood

The Underwood is quiet now.
No more rat-a-tat-tat-ta-tat – ding! – zzzip
His fingerprints may still be on those
old keys
some stuck down, some still up, ribbon twisted.
I am not inclined to wipe the dust.
It tells the story, of the passage of time
as it sits proudly, next to my modern computer.
I like to look at it while typing my poems.
It inspires me, and reminds me
of why I write words on paper
and paint pictures on canvas.
The Underwood is an instant memory
of the long black shiny table, stacks of books around it
the fountain pen, the clean white paper next to it
and the one fluttering out of the carriage
hanging on for dear life
as it sped side to side.
The physical, sometimes furious
rat-a-tat-tat-ta-tat – ding! –zzzip
rat-a-tat-tat-ta-tat – ding! –zzzip
I could hear it, in the early morning
late at night, hot summer afternoons
when he knew his thoughts would not be interrupted.
The sound comforted me, and made me curious
at those sporadic times during childhood
when I would stop long enough
to consider anything other than my own thoughts.
I wondered what the words were, and the stories
that were being punched out so passionately…
I know the words now, and I think about them
and him – the sound of the keys, like the train
like the rain, and time
racing by-
when I look at the Underwood.

-2002

4

Shadow

Walking
sun warm on my back
my shadow
in front of me.
I love to look
at my shadow.
Throughout my life
my shadow
has never changed.
Long and lean
young and hopeful
confidently moving forward
hair catching the breeze
and fluttering back
-a silhouette of
the real me.
Never sick
never tired
always new.
My thoughts
my dreams
my shadow.
As the sun comes up this morning
I look forward
to seeing me
again
today.

-2009

"Floating Oak" **acrylic on panel**

March

Black crows caw
sun warm on my face
white snow glares
sparkling in my sunglasses
water drips, red cardinals sing
promising spring
brown, crackle leaves hang from the maple
and especially from the oak in front.
Behind them, tightly furled, green leaves
are waiting to push through
now curled like fetuses
in red capped buds.
under the cold snow
warm buds grow
I can see them if I try
through my tinted eye
while drips drip
and winter cries
knowing he soon
dies.

-2003

"Franki" oil on panel

Looking for Spring

I love the sound of the birds
talking to each other in song
tree to tree
each with their own song of spring.
I'm on the deck
the sun shines through wispy clouds
snow covers most of the yard, after the nor'easter
but it is melting.
The sounds of dripping water, birds singing,
and the far away hum of cars on the highway.
The smell of melting snow and damp earth
and maybe even salt from the shore?
I love a tiny house, that pushes me out
to a big deck,
and a yard that borders the woods.
People who live in big houses, miss a lot I think.
Franceska just came out in her bathing suit,
side stepping the snow with her bare feet
to sit in her little chair, next to me.
She smells spring too!
She sits with her book, sunglasses and goose bumps.
We listen to birds, squirrels, chickens,
Dog chewing ice – crunch, crunch
we see buds on the very tops of some trees.
The quick thrill of the train approaching
here it comes! There it goes…
Then, it's gone
So nice that we can just sit here, while they race by.
The coming of a season, the exit of another
looking for spring.

2001

"The Winter Nest" **acrylic on panel**

Looking for Bats

When darkness begins to fall, in the early spring, and the sky is pearly blue,
I am on the studio east south-east facing deck, looking for bats.
Is it warm enough yet?
Over red budded trees is a fluorescent cloud –
floating slowly west. Unusual to be going that way – wind is usually from the east.
Crickets are chirping? Something is – maybe peepers?
Still no bats. I can see through swaying branches
over the cemetery. Bats do fly over cemeteries I have found.
Lots of open sky and bugs there. The little white cloud
-or more blue in the twilight-
has gone over the trees now, and another is coming-
still lit up against the darkening sky. I can smell the ocean in the wind
and hear a night bird. His song is so dramatic in this scene
-like an opera.
Stars are beginning to twinkle. Still no bats.
I guess it is too early in the season. Life is in the air though-
with the smells of green, soft brown earth and ocean white caps.
I will try again tomorrow
-looking for bats.

2006

"Winter's Gone" **acrylic on panel**

A flock of clouds
floated by.
One of them
caught my eye
and as it passed over me
I saw a robin in the tree.
As I looked up
he sang his song-
that spring is here
and winter's gone.

-2010

"Floating Leaf" acrylic on panel

Early Spring Rain

Gypsy and I are walking to the beach.
My shoes squeak because they are wet.
The air is heavy with water, and carries the scent of new life, and green.
Do I appreciate rain more, because my name is Drought?
The green seems to deepen every moment.
Raindrops ping on ivy and fallen leaves, and it is a beautiful sound.
There are lots of reflective puddles moving with rain,
and Gypsy must splash through each one
flicking water back from her paws as she jogs along
slurping out of some puddles, and chasing squirrels.
Saturated tree trunks, speckled green with lichen
have a lavender sheen, mixed with blue light, brown and sienna.
Hues of rust and light green dot the branches –
the promise of leaves to come.
Pass the cattails, more visible moving smoky-white sky and entering the beach.
Gypsy has her nose down constantly now
smelling the scents of all who have been here.
She sees the water. I let her off her leash, and she takes off
running on the deserted sand, zig zagging around invisible obstacles
playing her own game – picks up a piece of seaweed
and shakes it side to side.
I pick up a stick and hurl it into the water.
She gallops in, drinking splashes
but forgetting about the salt – cough! cough!
She swims to the stick, grabs it and swims back in
drops the stick, coughs and shakes, then grabs it again
and runs off, hoping I will chase her, but I don't.
I just look out at the horizon as the clouds run by…
After a few more throws, swims and shakes
the leash goes back on and off we go.
Gypsy needs some fresh water puddles to wash out the salt
and I am hoping she dries a little before we get back.
I am carrying a shell that I found on the beach
and Gypsy keeps trying to take it out of my hand
all the way home.

2004

12

Storm on the Marsh

Like a giant, dark winged Pegasus
beating its powerful wings
and pounding its hooves on the sky
a storm on the marsh
gallops through on the violet wind.
Flinging water and changing colors
plowing over bent sea grasses
-a dramatic romantic full spectrum
symphony!
And the gulls
riding on the wind
have front row seats.

2010

Yellow Dirt Road (Bauer Farm)

There is almost nothing
more romantic
than a winding dirt road.
Especially one that begins
at an historic farmhouse
curves around
a bridge covered lily pond
and up over a pastoral hill
by community gardens
then narrows
as it leads to a wooded
hiking path
as this one does.
It is always an adventure
to follow
the yellow dirt road.

2008

"Toad" **acrylic on panel**

Toad-ay

Toad-ay is a good day
to smell the green
to enjoy a blissful wooded scene
to feel the roots beneath my feet
the scent of flowers fresh and sweet.
Underneath the canopy
a busy web of harmony
spider robin toad and trees
fly stonewall moss and leaves
seasons change – an ebb and flow
summer autumn winter snow
today the moss is soft and warm
a small swirl of bugs to swarm
-a toad robin spider hunch
that spring is now serving lunch!

2011

"Green-Eyed Lady" acrylic on panel

Green Eyed Lady

As the windstorm blows
across the water
lavender white caps glow
against an ominous yellow sky.
Waves churn up the sand
mixing opaque brown with green seaweed
and lavender foam.
Then, unexpectedly
as the opaque wave curls
transparent, fluorescent
sea glass green light
shines through the wave top
like a watery eye-
thrilling, dramatic and fleeting
before the wave crashes on shore.
Salt spray
mixed with rain splashes
and windblown foam
explode
rhythmically
with both power and grace
as a giant green living beating
heart.

2010

"The Wave" **acrylic on panel**

Sea

At the end of the land
and the start of the sea
with my feet in the sand
-my breath full and free
as the sky reaches ocean
my mind and soul
-meet-
where there's peace
no commotion
here
I am complete.

- 2000

"Tuxis Clouds" **acrylic on canvas block**

Summer Morning

A pile of white clouds
sits
on an invisible shelf
above the horizon.
Teasing white sailboats tickle
the low, grey cloud-bellies
with their leaning masts
as they race by.
Watching steadily
I can see the clouds
exploding
higher and higher
into the bright blue sky.
White, grey, blue, pink, wind
and sun sparkle
on such a clear, playful
summer morning.

- 2002

19

"Tuxis Winter" **acrylic on canvas block**

Tuxis Island

This island, it intrigues me
for there, I've never been
and as I walk this path each day
the stories I can spin-
of summer island romance
beyond sight, just out of view
and secrets they are telling, so divine
I wish I knew!
Bottles may have washed ashore
with letters laced in sand
of couples in the throes of love
walking hand in hand.
Within the forest, between the trees
and echoes of woodpecker's peck
sits a cottage with a fireplace
grapes and goblets on the deck.
Then barefoot imprints lead
to a private little beach
on the other side, where I can't see
just beyond my reach...

-1999

"Translucent Shell" **acrylic on woodblock**

Translucent Shell

Walking on the beach
I encounter
a small, humble
shell from the sea
who
transmits sunlight
like a kaleidoscope
on a crystal stage
pinks, blues, cream
-what has this relic seen?
Smooth fragile treasure
is out of its element
if removed,
so I leave it
in the sand
alone
for the sun - the artist
To make it
glow.

-2012

Cape Cod

It's a mystical place, this arm in the sea
with rustic romance and history.
Dune walks yield sea relics I collect
with light-filled shadows, and color to reflect.
The driftwood, shells and feathers I've kept
just hold them in hand, and again, I'm swept-
away with the sea and the sand and the gulls
rhythmic reflections of rocking boat hulls
white houses on bluffs, bleached by days long
tan feet on worn wood
and the ocean's sweet song.

-1999

24

"Land & Sea" **oil on panel**

Sticks and Stones

Sticks and stones,
bleached shells and bones
-an ever changing sky-
muted grays cream and white
against a silent blue light
-an artful thing
to live
and die.

-2002

25

"Seaview Cloud" **oil on panel**

Beach Walk

On a clear, cool August evening
I walk on the beach road.
Children play in small yards.
Walkers and joggers pass me and smile or nod, and I do too.
The sky is still blue, although the sun is just going down.
Purple clouds and high, white clouds
hang, suspended
with orange and yellow highlights
over blue, reflective water
and white boats, glowing
in the last light of day.
As it gets darker, the sky and water are a lavender-blue
with iridescent clouds like holograms.
Sky and water merge, and it is hard to make out the horizon
but for the flickering lights of Long Island in the distance.
-a mass of lavender now with the whites of
the crescent moon, a lone cloud and boats
between beach houses.
Patio and porch lights are on, with torches and candles
and the smell of barbeques.
People are gathered, eating and talking
-each house having a different conversation
with gulls calling from Tuxis Island in the background.
They are gathering for the night too.
At the end of my walk, it is dark, violet, ultramarine blue
-almost black-
lights and televisions are on inside houses
and some porches are dark and quiet
while others continue.
There are no boats, water and sky to be seen anymore, tonight.
Streetlights are on, out-lighting the stars
as I get to my car.
After one last breath of the beach, sound of the waves, and look at the moon
I get in, start the engine, turn on my lights
and drive home.

-2000

"Barberry Hill Farm" detail – oil on canvas

Barberry Hill Farm

Comical sheep stand on rocks
that poke up out of the hillside meadow
like islands in the ocean
while white polar-bear sheep dogs
doze comfortably nearby.
Small lambs stand near ewes
both, not knowing
how the setting sun behind them
over the hillside
silhouettes their off-white, cloud-like wool
with a yellow halo
while their fluffy sides are bathed in gorgeous shadows
of blue and mauve.
Their noses and feet, touched with sienna
stand atop the fluorescent yellow-green grass
that they are munching.
At sunset, a tawny horse grazes, ready to follow chickens
to time-worn, comfortably warped white barns for the night
as the last slivers of light peek through.
While vegetables, fruit, flowers, wool, eggs, animals and trees
grow
another night takes over
and tired farmers get a well-earned rest.
The new day brings cars
driving by on Route 1
getting a last glimpse of a country farm
before banking the curve to town
and golfers on the tee see the stand come together again
with the bounty of the farm
and the beauty
of hard labor that looks easy.
The art of the earth is on display
as the first car stops
to share the harvest.

-1999

29

"Grace Cottage" oil on panel

Grace Cottage

A pocketful of shells
and smooth stones.
A tiny, lone cedar sways in the breeze.
Weathered wood, creaking stairs
small footprints go
from the door to the shore
blue reflections from the sky
rhythmic sparkles passing by
waves dependably land
on mauve brown, wet sand
-quiet days like these
and scented blonde beach grass
blow
like a child's hair
through the wind
of my dreams.

- 2012

"Rain Coming" **oil on panel**

Summer Rain

Pinging
off forest floor
leaves and rocks.
Drizzling
down lichen laced
mauve tree trunks.
Disappearing
into brown dirt
moving waves, beach sand and
greedy green grass.
Plunking
into rising lush streams
and scattered street puddles.
Other drops – so small
they form
a sultry summer mist
and hang in the air
moist on my face
and fragrant sea musk in my nose
that is the scent of life itself
-the gift of green-
a summer rain.

-2009

"Old Red" **oil on panel**

The Mortgage

My clothes
hang on me
like a warm, wet towel.
Thunderhead clouds
pile up
on the south western
horizon.
If the mortgage was paid
I would love the excitement
of the instability in the atmosphere
-the rising
of the thunderheads
-the pinks, blues, yellows
swirling upward
into a distant blue mist
darkening sky
impending thunder
welcome rain...
But
with the mortgage unpaid
all I see
is
-the bugs-

-2012

"Super Moon" **acrylic on panel**

Witness

Walking to see the super moon.
Down the road where old trees have exposed roots
like huge elderly hands gripping the last
real earth before the pavement.
To the beach road
big houses on both sides create a tunnel.
The bridge where marsh opens up and
light rains down on lush green marsh grass purple mud, egrets,
and fence creek sunset to the west,
and moonrise to the east
expected over the Sound, but no moon yet just blue haze.
I wonder if I will see it.
Over the hill houses overlook the road facing south
each has its own wood walk over the wetland
and the dune, to the beach.
From here I can see the whole sky, east to west.
Winding around inroads, about half hour and a mile later
back to the bridge. No moon yet.
Through the tunnel and to East Wharf Beach and
see people looking east-
THERE IT IS.
A huge yellow orange ball rising above the horizon
into the blue..
I must see it from the bridge
So I jog back there and it is a bit higher and brighter
others are there taking pictures.
I just stand there breathing, and looking.
We are all quiet.
Eventually, I go back the way I came
pass the elder trees, and now hear crickets
peepers and see bats against the twilight sky
looking over my shoulder between houses to see the moon.
The last thing I see before getting to my car
are 2 boys riding bikes down the road
going toward the shore, past me and one has a black tee shirt
that says "WITNESS" in big white letters.

-8/10/2014

"Equinox Moon" **acrylic on panel**

Equinox Moon

The deep greens of late summer
are still in the trees,
but the marsh grass
glows
with autumn fire colors
on this equinox evening.
The big, bright, full moon
appears
rising over the haze
into pink atmosphere
giving everything a romantic halo.
The scent of the ocean
and moist, end-of-summer breeze
swim together in my nose
and become-
a summer beach memory
-of tan feet in the sand,
sound of the waves,
warm afternoon conversations,
sunny long days
and moonlit evenings
like this.

-2010

"Field Of Dreams" **acrylic on panel**

Field of Dreams

It is late afternoon –
early October, John Lennon's birthday
-to the small, humble field near my house.
Through the break in the white pines
like through the corn stalks in the movie,
"Field of Dreams".
I can see the field stretch out to the east
to meet tall oaks and maple trees
near the tracks.
The train rumbles by. The sky is changing
to cerulean green.
The street light goes on.
The crescent moon begins to show.
The peepers begin their chorus.
Shadow is crawling across the field
and – slowly – up the trees
that are just beginning to turn fall colors.
As the sun line heads to the top
It looks like – *a hearth fire*
like a dream
and maybe it was, as the flame goes out
and shadow takes over…
Bathed in moonlit cobalt twilight
I gather my paints and paint sketch
and disappear through the pines
toward home
from dream to reality.

-2010

"October Marsh" **acrylic on panel**

October Marsh

In the late afternoon
of a brilliant, crisp, autumn day
on Seaview Avenue
the sun dips behind beach houses
and the shadow covers half the marsh
-I don't know which is more beautiful-
the florescent light igniting
the changing colors of the marsh grass, cottages and maples
or
the warm rust, burgundy and amber
of the encroaching shadow
that will soon encompass the scene.
Each
makes the other magnificent
in this brief moment
on the October marsh.

-2010

"Oak Moon" oil on panel

October Moonlight Walk

I jog to catch up with people in the dark. Bagpipe whines,
through misty moonlight, before I get to the trail.
I look up in the open, green meadow, over my shoulder
and see clouds, rushing by a huge harvest moon. Catch up to the group
of bobbing flashlights, and fall into place behind the last one,
into the wooded doorway.
The air is damp, musty and earthy
with the smells of
trees and moss, and a hint of the sea.
I touch the cedars, and feel like a druid.
Bagpipes wail in the distance
I look down at my feet lit by my flashlight.
The trail changes
from roots, to rocks and sand, to moss, to wood walks over wetlands.
People are talking softly, about common things
but I am not, because I am alone, with wet breath.
We go up a hill and all stop around the bagpiper, listening,
looking up in the clearing, at the perfect view of the moon.
The bagpiper goes on and we follow, and loop back to the original trail.
It all takes less than an hour, but seems like longer, and I don't want it to end.
Some go in for cider, but I don't. I want to stay, alone
for a while longer, and look at the moon
and smell the moist salty sea earth air
before going home.

-2002

Shoreline Shakespeare

When I see a storm, like a giant, rolling comma
racing north over New England
on the weather map
I know that it is a beach day!
Stampeding clouds, like a herd of black buffalo
on the plains, run across the sky, on the wind.
Green waves are thrown onto the sand
and foam spreads out, like a white banner
pulled in and thrown out again, like dough under a giant rolling pin.
Seagulls are everywhere, in between clouds, lighting the whitecaps,
competing with expert aerodynamics, feathers ruffling
hovering, suspended, bright white boomerangs against the dark
and moving sky, surfing on the gusts.
A delicate, but daring butterfly
tumbles past on the wind, like an autumn leaf.
The gulls, the monarch and I
are the only ones in this theater, right now, and it is a shame
because, if all the world is a stage
then today, right here,
nature is Shakespeare!

-2003

"Wharf Storm" **oil on panel**

"November Shore" **acrylic on panel**

November Shore

So quiet, peaceful, one
welcome warmth of midday sun
whispering yellow cattails hum
twin beach houses, sleepy, hollow
crystal waves lapping shallow
colored rocks and shells below
so tempting, my hand must go
plunging into clear and cold
to touch the smooth inviting glow
cool soft sand under toes
fresh clean scent in my nose
from the Sound, from the sea
to Circle Beach
and home with me.

-2011

"November Moon" 5 by 7 oil on panel

"November Moon" **acrylic on panel**

November Moon

Down my quiet lane
haunting moan of the passing train
nostrils sucking in
the scents of wet leaves and earth rise
out, as moist mist, clouding my eyes.
Follow the trunks of oaks up high
between, a brilliant twilight sky
to sparse leaves of brown and maroon
around a brightening half moon...
as scent, sound, sight and time collide
I think of dawn rising on the other side
and, as this moonlight comes to me
I think of them, and what
they see.

-2007

"Oak Leaves and Root" oil on panel

November Woods

Low afternoon sun
fires orange
through a warm prism of leaves
still clinging to a young tree
in the November woods.
A doe
stepping through
almost invisible
almost silent
-crackle of a dry twig-
pricks her ears, turns her head, sees her breath.
Grey sky moves in overhead
yellow afternoon light
turns to grey-blue twilight.
Cold white flakes begin to fall
quietly
through indigo air
and land
on soft warm backs
bare brown branches
red forest floor.
-at this moment-
as day turns to night
autumn turns to winter.

-2009

"Cape Fantasy" acrylic on panel

A Winter Fantasy

Out on the Cape, an artist furlough
off to the windswept town of Truro!
A small beach house on a dune
a winter-light afternoon – other shacks are in sight,
but far away, with flickering lights.
Warm, wood floor, rugs, and a little T.V.
cute kitchen, food, an old movie
coffee, red wine, candles, white socks
worn sneakers for walking
stone hearth, wood box.
A crooked rustic broom for sweeping sand
leans against the stone like an elderly hand
-upstairs-
big bed, soft blankets, fluffy pillows with seams
worn sweatshirts and jeans hang from hooks on old beams.
An easel, French doors, a small balcony
overlooking the dunes and the endless sea...
With north view skylights looking up
scattered paints, wet brushes in a chipped clay cup
paper, pens galore, an old wooden desk
-a lovely, artistic, dream of a mess.
-downstairs-
after a star-lit night,
waking, by chance, to first morning light
on the eastern horizon, a rising, red flare
just me, a big deck, and Atlantic air!
Dune grass sweeps the railing stairs to wood-walk, then to beach
last stair, sand buried, with my bare feet.
Sipping morning coffee in my hand
looking out to sea – the day, a plan-
driftwood, feathers, hunting for treasure,
painting shadows, finding words, just for pleasure
no time, but light, day turns to night,
morning, noon, twilight, dawn, telling time with no watch on.
This is my winter fantasy and today
I will keep it close to me.

-2002

53

"Snowstorm Coming" **oil on panel**

Snowstorm Coming

I can smell it – moist and clean
it hovers
see the veil as it covers
far blue hills, barns with hay
dormant fields
comes this way
flakes are falling- the veil arrives
grey clumps against white sky
down to trees
grass
where I stand
snow is now everywhere
and even
on my hair.

-2005

"Snow" **acrylic on panel**

Snow

Sky falling
around and down
in no rush to find the ground
my warm-breath cloud
thudding boot sound
-I stop-
what if my boots were roots
and I could be
as this tree?
In silence
truth is here
it whispers in my ear...
flakes swirl
float land
and turn to tears
upon my hand.

-2010

Winter Cottage

Winter cottage, are you resting
echoing icecap waves to hear?
The howl of a cold nor'easter
whistling at your wood-wall ear?
Snow glare from your frosted windows
sparkles on a blue horizon.
An empty clothesline, simple, bare
outdoor shower with chrome-snow hair.
One sea gull soars above your roof
-a sign of summer past and proof
that although the cold still holds tight
time will bring summer's light
to melt the snow and warm the sand
life to house, again, will land.
The shower pour, the clothesline flutter
warm towels, grille and sailboat rudder...
Dream on, cottage, in winter sleep
A summer promise, you must keep.

- 2001

A Sliver of Light

on a clear
cold
dark
winter solstice night
along the edge of the moon
over a grove
of tall, strong, sleeping
oak trees
evergreens
with the blue glow
of sun
still on the horizon
gives hope-
that the sun is rising
on the other side
in another's eyes
and every new day
brings us closer
to
Peace on Earth.

2001

"Winter Field" **acrylic on canvas black**

Burning Brooms

At mid-winter twilight
the orange light ignites
the bare tree tops
and they look like
upside-down burning brooms.
The orange flame turns red
as the line moves up
the sun goes down
the flame goes out
and leaves
a quiet blue night
with light snow
falling...

- 2002

Take My Hand

Take my hand, and let us walk
and all fall silent, as we talk.
Through our touch, a vow we give
to hold this hand, as we live.
The path before us, smooth and clear
but up ahead, it disappears.
We know not what we will find
-it twists and turns. We walk blind.
But, even in the darkest night
in desert hot or blinding light
we feel the hand that keeps us strong
through thorn and thicket, joyous song.
In frigid forest winter's frost
with piles of snow, the path is lost.
Our hands warmth pulses through
and cuts a path behind us, new.
Under oceans green and mountains high
as days and time and years go by
our hands joined are one and so
I'm blessed this day,
for this, I know-
no gift on earth, on sea or land
is
as finding you, to take my hand.

- 2001

It

It
is the pure
treasured memory
of the past
passionate
romance.

It
is the ember
that glows
in the paintings
and the poems
and gives them
life.

It
is the desire
the longing
to re-live
the love
that was.

It
is the spark
the penetrating
intensity
the vulnerability
and total surrender
in those
beautiful
blue eyes
looking at me.

- 2008

"Self Portrait" **oil on canvas**

The Mirror

Sometimes I fear, I'm lost in the mirror
and there is no substance to me.
I'm just a reflection of somebody else
and not my own entity.
The reflections of those, that I hold dear
are guilt in these words, I don't want to hear-
the frustration of an invisible tear...
The tear is not wet and salty to feel
maybe nothing about me is real-
I'm a means to an end that I cannot see
In the now flash the future, and history
like a frequency others cannot hear
the message is there, but still unclear...
I have to face the ghost in the mirror
and
hold on tight
so I don't disappear.

- 2000

The Room

There is a room.
It is empty, round and small
and has no doors or windows.
Loud bold printed wallpaper screams out at me
from the wall
in a repetitive pattern
over and over
as I walk around the room
searching
for a hole, a door, a window, a crack, anything!
There is none.
The ceiling is high, clear, thick glass
I can see the sky and eternal freedom
above.
The cloud formations, ever-changing
without responsibility or care
or even destination
passing by, darkening, raining, electrifying
thundering, disappearing, reappearing, floating
while-I-go-in-circles.
My neck hurts from looking up
and I must look at the loud wallpaper again.
Even if I cover my eyes and ears
my hands like a vice on my skull
pounding through my head like a drum
boom-boom-BOOM-BOOM!
Around and around and around
until someday I will fall
and die
in this room.

- 2000

I love-

The tiny ant walking by
the spider, whose web I spy
the butterfly, an artful sight
the firefly, who lights the night
the luna moth, who glows bright
the peepers peeping in late spring
the birds, in early morning, sing
the talking crows caw tree to tree
the toad who I can hardly see
the red tailed hawk, soars high and free
the fox & skunk, at a distance, love
the cooing of the morning dove
the crossing frog, on a rainy day
the redwing blackbird, so much to say
the raccoon, with its human hands
the ancient oak's acorn lands
the weeping willow in wet lands
the apple trees, with apples, red
the tomatoes in the garden bed
the maple's orange and crimson leaves
the bat hanging in the eves
the wolf's howl on the plains
the desert's rare and welcome rains
the river, that winds its way through
and empties into ocean blue
the whale's moan, haunting, low
the turtle's life, zen-ly slow
the mountains who touch the sky
the storm clouds passing by
the snow that peacefully lands
on yellow fields, and my hands
the sun that shines warm on me
and gives life its energy
the earth, our home, I love her most
our blue and green mother host
all the earth and all the sky
and all who walk, swim and fly
I will love, until I die.

-2014

"Hermit Crab and the Minnow" **Crayola markers and Sharpie pen**

HERMIT CRAB & THE MINNOW

In the shallow waters of the low tide, there were hermit crabs, snails, minnows, seaweed, rocks and shells of all colors and shapes. Minnows darted in and out of seaweed in flashes of orange and green. Hermit crabs scurried around, kicking up sand, while slimy slow snails clung to rocks with no worry about time.

There was, however, one hermit crab who was very still. He moved only to get food and then quickly hid inside his shell and stayed there, looking like a plain grey stone. There was also one curious minnow who noticed the quiet crab and broke free of her little school of minnows to try to talk to him.

She appeared early one morning, and gently tapped on his shell with her little green fin.

"Hello in there. Is anyone home?"

"No!" said the hermit crab.

"Someone must have said 'no'…," laughed the Minnow. "Why don't you come out?"

"Because I don't want to… now, go away!" he shouted. The Minnow swam away, but she returned later that day.

"Hello again," she said. "The sun is out and its rays are shining in the water across all of the different colored rocks, making them glow! You should see it."

"No," said the hermit crab, "I do not wish to come out." The Minnow quietly swam off.

The next morning, she was back again!

"What do you see inside your shell?" she asked the hermit crab.

"It is grey with a black stripe," he said slowly. Then after a moment he asked, "Is it sunny out today?"

"No," the Minnow smiled, "It is cloudy and the water is a very peaceful purple. You should see it!"

"I can't." he said. "I am afraid."

The Minnow thought for a moment, and then she said excitedly, "Maybe, if you put one leg out every day, you could get used to it!"

"I don't know... I don't know if I can..."

"I think you can." the Minnow said, and she turned and darted back to her school.

The next day when the Minnow arrived, sure enough, Hermit Crab had one leg sticking out of his shell.

"You have one leg out!" she cried.

Each day when the minnow came back in the morning, Hermit Crab had another leg out, and each day she told him about all of the wonderful sights that he would soon see.

Finally, the day came when all of Hermit Crabs' legs were out, and only his head remained inside his shell, and the minnow came to him.

"Today is the day you will put your head out!" she said.

"I don't know if I can." he said. "I am very frightened..."

"Oh, but if you put your head out, and open your eyes, you will see something very special," she said. "It is orange and shimmering green and has a very nice smile..."

And with that, Hermit Crab popped his head out and saw the beautiful Minnow.

"You did it!" she cried.

Hermit Crab opened his eyes wide, as he never had before... and he saw all of the dazzling wonders around him. The rest of that day, and every day after, Hermit Crab and the Minnow enjoyed the sights of the shallow waters together. Through the eyes and words of the Minnow, Hermit Crab had a new and magical view of the world around him. He was very lucky to have a friend like the Minnow.... she helped him to "see".   The End

Sara Drought Nebel 1996

"Toad" Crayola markers and Sharpie pen

TOAD & ROBIN

Toad lived in a perfect place in the small woods, near the wise, ancient maple, the moss-covered old stone wall and the forgotten pond. He was virtually invisible in his stillness and camouflage, observing all that grew, hopped, swam, flew and crawled around him.

One warm, early spring day, a robin landed nearby, one who Toad had seen before, searching for worms near where Toad was sitting, on the old stone wall. She ran, zig zagging back and forth in the leaves, near the moss and roots of the ancient maple, stopping every so often to listen...

Without warning, she suddenly landed on the stone wall right in front of Toad! This startled him, but he stayed still. She cocked her head, looked at him and said,

"You are very ugly, aren't you?"

"I don't know.." answered Toad slowly, "I've never thought about what I look like.. Am I ugly?"

"Yes, you surely are!" she said, matter of factly, "You are very ugly. I wish you were smaller so I could eat you, but you probably wouldn't taste very good anyway."

With that, she abruptly flew back down to continue looking for worms.

Toad thought about what she had just said. With all of the creatures that he had seen, he had never considered any to be ugly. Each was interesting in its own way. Even the bugs he ate, he thought were beautiful. Whether they crawled, flew or swam, he was thankful that they were there for him to eat, and look at and think about.

A couple of days later, on a breezy, rainy day, he saw the robin again, and she spoke to him,

"Don't you go anywhere else, or are you too afraid? Maybe you are too lazy to go anywhere? Why do you just sit here all the time?"

Toad did not know how to answer her. Why would he go anywhere else when this place had everything he needed or wanted, and anything he wanted to eat came to him in good time? He loved to be still and think, and watch the creatures around him, and he thought about the things the robin said long after she was gone.

A few days later, on a cool, sunny day, she was back with a bunch of other robins, and she and two others flew up to the wall.

"See, of course he is still here. Didn't I tell you that he was ugly?"

"Oh yes!" the other robins laughed, "He is the ugliest thing ever, and he can't even fly!"

"But I can swim…" said Toad slowly, but the robins had already flown off, not waiting for a response.

Just when Toad thought he would not see Robin again, one warm, mid-summer late morning, he heard a strange, whimpering tweet, near the break in the stone wall, and he hopped over to see what this unfamiliar noise was. It was Robin, and she was hurt. Her wing was bent a little, and her head was bleeding.

"What happened?" asked Toad.

"I am not sure", she said, "I was flying near that house over there and hit something hard that I didn't see… My head hurts and I can't fly, and there is a cat at that house and I am afraid that it will come and eat me! I thought you would be here… can you help me?"

Toad thought and thought. He thought about what he knew about birds and cats, and the woods where he lived. Then, from his place on the wall, he could see the cat sniffing around near the edge of the woods, in the distance.

"I have an idea," he said, "but we must hurry, as I can see the cat from here."

"Oh, no!" she cried, "what will I do?!"

Toad hopped down and told Robin to follow him. He led her to the forgotten pond.

"I can't swim!" Robin cried. "Why did you bring me here?!"

"I CAN swim", said Toad, "now carefully get on my back." She did. Toad swam her to the center of the pond, where an old beaver-built log pile stuck out of the water. He told Robin to get off of his back and onto the log pile.

"Why? Are you sure it will hold me? I don't trust you!"

"Trust me," said Toad, "I've lived here all of my life. I knew the beavers who built this and it is a good, sturdy place. I also know that cats do not like to swim, so you'll be safe here."

So, Robin got onto the log pile and Toad began to swim away.

"Hey, where are you going? You aren't going to leave me here are you?!"

"No, " said Toad, "I am going to get twigs, grass and moss to build you a nest and bugs and worms for you to eat so you can heal. I will be right back."

Toad swam back and forth for the rest of the day and into the night, to build Robin's nest and then brought two moths for her dinner. Every day he brought meals, and her favorite-worms- when he could get them, and watched over her. The cat did come by two or three times and circled the pond, but since he refused to get wet, he gave up and did not return.

One still, sunny morning in early autumn, Robin was feeling much better.

"Toad," she said, after a breakfast of a tasty worm and a mosquito, "I think I would like to try flying. Would you swim me to shore?"

"Of course," said Toad, but when Robin hopped onto Toad's back, he strained under her increased weight, and his weight loss... He made it, barely, and when she got off onto the bank, he breathed a sigh of relief! He hoped he would not have to do that again! Robin stretched and preened her wings and after a few tries, got herself to the stone wall, and then, by early afternoon, to a low limb on the ancient maple. Then she flew short distances, until she was very confident in her flying.

"Will you be going away now?" asked Toad, softly.

"YES!" said Robin excitedly. "My family will be so worried and so happy to see me! Goodbye!" She flew off.

Toad watched her disappear through the trees. He sat in the quiet stillness of the afternoon on the rock where he had first met Robin, and thought about her. He watched the light change as the afternoon went by, and eventually, a tear began to trickle down his bumpy cheek...

Right before sunset, Robin returned. "I almost forgot to thank you," she said. "Thank you for saving me... well, I must get back now!"

But right before she took off again, Toad asked, "Robin... do you still think that I am ugly?"

Robin, who had not noticed before, saw the glint of the tear glistening on his cheek. "Oh, no", she said, "you are not ugly... I was wrong. You are beautiful, and this place is beautiful, and you belong here... Goodbye Toad, and thank you again!" And, in a feathery fluster, she was gone.

Toad looked around, at the ancient maple, the forgotten pond, the magical sliver of last-light on the moss covered old stone wall where he was sitting, the brilliant orange and red autumn foliage, and the peepers began their evening song... he felt totally happy, warm and peaceful inside. As the blue twilight of night washed over the woods - a mosquito, moth AND a fly became his dinner... this was the first meal in a long time that he did not have to share, and it was LOVELY!

The End

Sara Drought Nebel 2011

"Robin" **acrylic on panel**

"Self Portrait" **Pencil**

Sara Drought Nebel, poet and award-winning painter, was educated at Bennington College, Bennington, VT and Silvermine Guild, New Canaan, CT

She paints and shows with the CT Plein Air Painters Society, the New Haven Paint & Clay Club, the Lyme Art Association, and local art groups when not out on her own finding small earthscapes to paint in and around, the beach, the woods, and her (Treefort) studio in Madison, CT.

Paintings and portraits are in public and private collections throughout the northeast, and can be seen in juried shows along the CT Shoreline, on her web site, local galleries – William Pitt Sotheby's International Realty's Madison (670 Boston Post Rd.) and Guilford (73 Church St.) offices, and by appointment at the Treefort Studio & Gallery, where she lives, works, and teaches art classes for teenagers and adults. Biography is listed in *Who's Who in America 2002*

A Sliver of Light – Meditations- Paintings, Poems & Stories, is Sara's second book. See her website to visit the store (books, cards, organic cotton tees, totes & posters), and to find information about paintings, classes, exhibits, seasonal Open Studio Sundays and events. Witness Earth (walk) conversations are on facebook, twitter, pinterest and tumblr.

www.justplainart.com
www.justplainart.tumblr.com
www.twitter.com/justplainart
www.pinterest.com/justplainart
www.facebook.com/justplainart

Printed in the United States
By Bookmasters